Little Pebble™

AUG 2 0 2019

Mammals in the Wild

Hippopotamuses
A 4D BOOK

by Kathryn Clay

PEBBLE
a capstone imprint

Download the Capstone app!

- Ask an adult to download the Capstone 4D app.

- Scan the cover and stars inside the book for additional content.

When you scan a spread, you'll find fun extra stuff to go with this book! You can also find these things on the web at www.capstone4D.com using the password: hippos.00795

Pebble Books are published by Pebble
1710 Roe Crest Drive, North Mankato,
Minnesota 56003
www.mycapstone.com

Library of Congress Cataloging-in-Publication Data
Names: Clay, Kathryn, author.
Title: Hippopotamuses : a 4D book / by Kathryn Clay.
Description: North Mankato, Minnesota : an imprint of Pebble, [2019] |
  Series: Little Pebble. Mammals in the wild | Audience:
  Age 4–7.
Identifiers: LCCN 2018004131 | ISBN 9781977100917
  (eBook PDF) | ISBN 9781977100795 (hardcover) | ISBN
  9781977100856 (paperback)
Subjects: LCSH: Hippopotamidae—Juvenile literature.
Classification: LCC QL737.U57 C55 2019 | DDC
  599.63/5—dc23
LC record available at https://lccn.loc.gov/2018004131

Editorial Credits
Karen Aleo, editor; Juliette Peters, designer;
Tracy Cummins and Heather Mauldin, media researchers;
Laura Manthe, production specialist

Photo Credits
Getty Images: Beverly Joubert, 19, Marco Pozzi Photographer, 15; Shutterstock: AlenaPo, Design Element, Andrew Linscott, 17, boyphare, 5, Hailin Chen, 9, Johan Swanepoel, Cover, Karel Bartik, 1, Markovka, Design Element, Netta Arobas, 21, Photo Africa SA, 11, Volodymyr Burdiak, 7; Thinkstock: Stockbyte, 13

Printed in the United States of America.
PA021

Table of Contents

Up Close

Grunt! Snort!

A hippopotamus rests.

Yawn!

Its large mouth opens.

See the sharp teeth.

A hippo has short legs.

It has a heavy body.

But it runs fast.

Hippos are mammals.

They breathe air.

On Water and Land

Hippos go in rivers.

They don't swim.

They walk under the water.

Hippos walk on land.

This hippo sweats.

The sweat looks like blood!

Hippos live in groups.
They rest in the mud
or water.

Time to Eat

The sun goes down.

It's time to eat.

Hippos find grass.

A calf is born.

It drinks milk.

Soon it will eat grass too.

Glossary

blood—the liquid that the heart pumps through the body

breathe—to take air in and out of the lungs

calf—a young hippo

mammal—a warm-blooded animal that breathes air; mammals have hair or fur; female mammals feed milk to their young

snort—a short, rough sound made through the nose

sweat—liquid that comes out of the skin to protect the skin

Read More

Borgert-Spaniol, Megan. *Baby Hippos.* Blastoff Readers: Super Cute! Minneapolis: Bellwether Media, 2016.

DiSiena, Laura Lyn, and Hannah Eliot. *Hippos Can't Swim and Other Fun Facts.* Did You Know? New York: Little Simon, 2014.

London, Jonathan. *Hippos are Huge!* Read and Wonder. Somerville, Mass.: Candlewick Press, 2015.

Internet Sites

Use FactHound to find Internet sites related to this book.

Visit www.facthound.com

Just type in 9781977100795 and go.

Check out projects, games and lots more at
www.capstonekids.com

Critical Thinking Questions

1. Where do hippos live?

2. How do hippos breathe in the water?

3. What do baby hippos eat?

Index